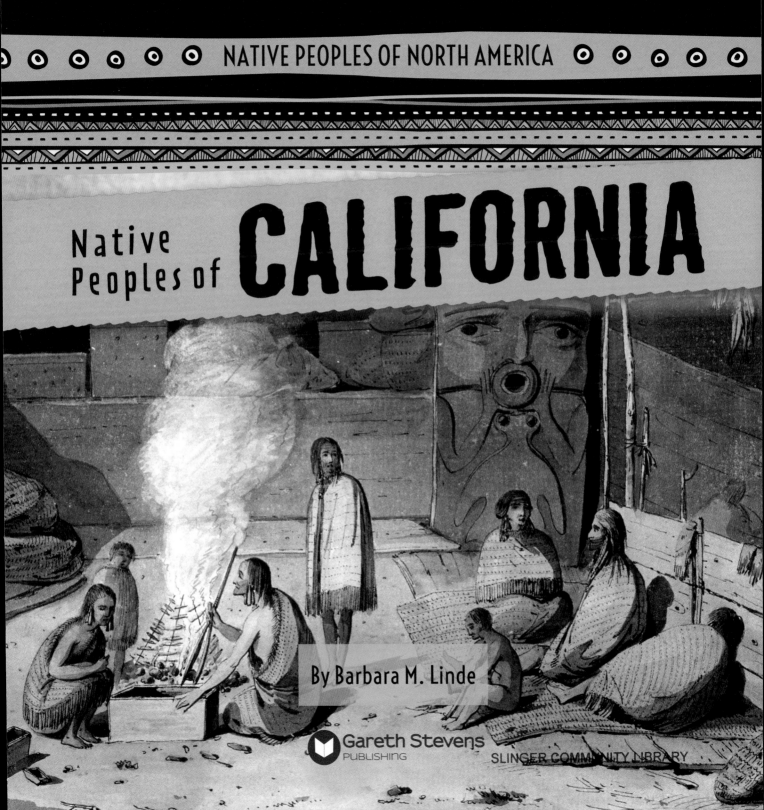

Native Peoples of CALIFORNIA

By Barbara M. Linde

Gareth Stevens
PUBLISHING

Please visit our website, www.garethstevens.com. For a free color catalog of all our high-quality books, call toll free 1-800-542-2595 or fax 1-877-542-2596.

Library of Congress Cataloging-in-Publication Data

Names: Linde, Barbara M., author.
Title: Native peoples of California / Barbara M. Linde.
Description: New York : Gareth Stevens Publishing, 2017. | Series: Native peoples of North America | Includes index.
Identifiers: LCCN 2015050138 | ISBN 9781482448238 (pbk.) | ISBN 9781482448092 (library bound) | ISBN 9781482447590 (6 pack)
Subjects: LCSH: Indians of North America–California–History–Juvenile literature.
Classification: LCC E78.C15 L55 2017 | DDC 979.4004/97–dc23
LC record available at http://lccn.loc.gov/2015050138

First Edition

Published in 2017 by
Gareth Stevens Publishing
111 East 14th Street, Suite 349
New York, NY 10003

Designer: Samantha DeMartin
Editor: Kristen Nelson

Photo credits: Series art AlexTanya/Shutterstock.com; cover, p. 1 DEA Picture Library/De Agostini/Getty Images; p. 5 (background) Mariusz S. Jurgielewicz/Shutterstock.com; p. 5 (map) AlexCovarrubias/Wikimedia Commons; p. 7 (top left) Tom Grundy/Shutterstock.com; p. 7 (top right) Ysbrand Cosijn/Shutterstock.com; p. 7 (bottom left) Radoslaw Lecyk/Shutterstock.com; p. 7 (bottom right) Andrew Zarivny/Shutterstock.com; p. 9 David McNew/Getty Images News/ Getty Images; p. 11 (inset) Print Collector/Hulton Archive/Getty Images; p. 11 (main) Science & Society Picture Library/ SSPL/Getty Images; p. 13 (main) Education Images/Universal Images Group/Getty Images; p. 13 (inset) Bobbi Onia/ Underwood Archives/Archive Photos/Getty Images; pp. 15, 17 Buyenlarge/Archive Photos/Getty Images; p. 19 Nativestock.com/Marilyn Angel Wynn/Nativestock/Getty Images; p. 21 Mike Baird/Wikimedia Commons; p. 23 Fototeca Storica Nazionale./Hulton Archive/Getty Images; p. 25 Ralph Crane/The LIFE Picture Collection/ Getty Images; p. 27 courtesy of the Environmental Protection Agency; p. 29 (top left) Mel Melcon/Los Angeles Times/ Getty Images; p. 29 (top right, bottom left) Toni Ard/Moment Mobile/Getty Images; p. 29 (bottom right) Photo Researchers/Science Source/Getty Images.

Printed in the United States of America

CPSIA compliance information: Batch #CS16GS: For further information contact Gareth Stevens, New York, New York at 1-800-542-2595.

CONTENTS

Words in the glossary appear in **bold** type the first time they are used in the text.

The Way to CALIFORNIA

Did you know people first came to California over 10,000 years ago? They found a land with plenty of water, sunshine, and food. The weather was not too hot or too cold.

Archaeologists have different ideas about when and how the first people came to California. They know some **migrated** from Asia across a land bridge and then traveled south to California. They think others traveled by boat from islands in the Pacific Ocean. Perhaps more groups came from the east across the mountains or up from the south.

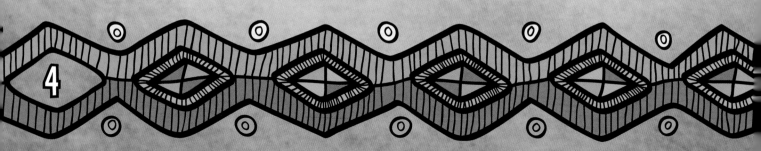

Since there are no written records, we may never know for sure exactly when the first peoples arrived or where they came from. Still, archaeologists keep looking for clues.

Greenland

Canada

United States

Mexico

☐ = where the native peoples of California lived

TELL ME MORE

The Pacific Ocean lies to the west of California. People who lived in California used it for food and travel.

The Geography of CALIFORNIA

California has a rocky coast to the west. High mountains called the Sierra Nevada are in the east. A large desert runs across the south. Because of the land's features, groups of native peoples commonly found one area to settle in. They didn't need to move around much, since food and water were plentiful in most of California. Supplies for houses were easy to find, too.

Most groups' lands had natural **boundaries** respected by other native peoples. There wasn't much fighting between groups.

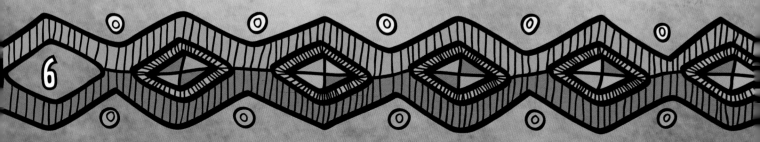

Most groups named themselves their word for "people." They named other groups by where they lived.

Before Europeans arrived, California had about 1 million native peoples living in the dry desert, on the coast, and in the foothills of the Sierra Nevada.

7

CReation STORIES

Here are two creation stories of native Californians:

The Yokut believed the eagle and the coyote were on a small piece of land surrounded by water. They sent the turtle to bring back soil from the bottom of the water. From this, they made a large earth and six men and six women.

The Chumash believed the earth goddess Hutash made people from magic seeds. They lived on an island. Hutash made a rainbow bridge so the people could cross to the **mainland**.

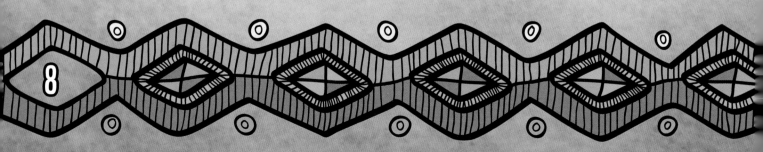

Both the Yokut and Chumash people drew pictographs, or rock drawings, like this one. Some of what historians know about them comes from these.

TELL ME MORE

The native peoples spoke over 80 languages. Members of one group wouldn't commonly be able to understand people from other groups.

Beautiful BASKETS

How did California's native peoples carry or store their things? They made baskets! Small baskets held medicines and seeds. Large cooking baskets were made so they didn't **leak** and could be used to make soup. The cook put hot stones in the soup and stirred it until it was cooked. Basket traps caught birds and fish. Babies stayed safe in cradle baskets.

The baskets were made with wood, plants, beads, bones, and skins. Some baskets were covered with feathers or shells. Others had **designs** on them.

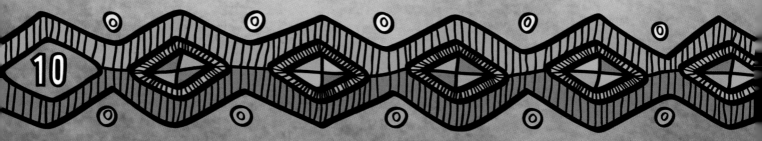

The native peoples in California were hunters and gatherers. They used their baskets to gather what they needed, such as grass seed and acorns.

TELL ME MORE

The California State Parks has a collection of 3,000 Indian baskets. You can see them at the State Indian Museum or look at some of them online!

11

The SALINAN

Since the Salinan (suh-LEE-nuhn) people lived near the water, they ate fish and water birds, though they hunted other animals, too. Acorns, berries, seeds, and greens were important foods for them to gather.

Salinan babies stayed in a cradle that was tied to their mother's back. Children played games that were like modern soccer and field hockey. Boys learned to hunt with bows and arrows. They also learned to dance and sing. Girls helped gather food, cook, and take care of the family.

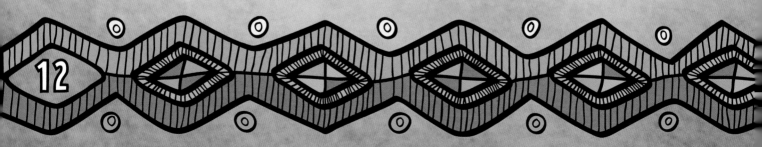

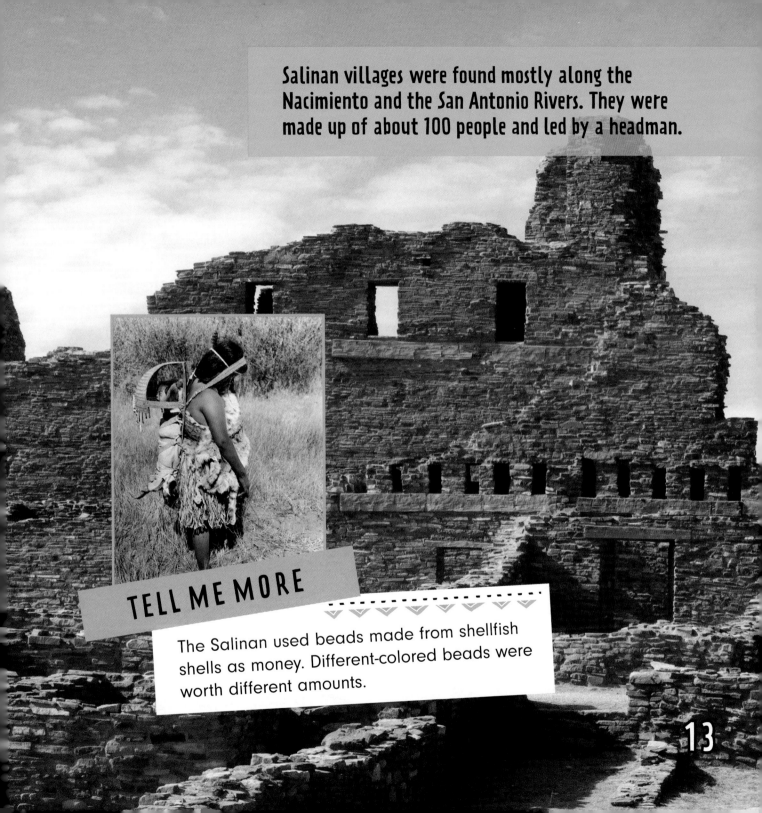

Salinan villages were found mostly along the Nacimiento and the San Antonio Rivers. They were made up of about 100 people and led by a headman.

TELL ME MORE

The Salinan used beads made from shellfish shells as money. Different-colored beads were worth different amounts.

The MIWOK

A Miwok (MEE-wahk) village might have from about 24 to a few hundred people. Each village was independent, but sometimes villages traded or worked together.

Like other native groups of California, the Miwok wasted very little. When hunters caught a deer, everyone ate the meat. They then made deerskin clothing, and the bones were used for tools. Plants were used as food, to make brushes, and to make soap. Acorns were ground up and mixed with water to make a tasty mush or soup.

In Indian Grinding Rock State Historic Park in California, you can see the places the Miwok ground acorns. Acorns were one of the most important foods for native peoples living in California.

TELL ME MORE

Miwok people danced to give thanks, pray, and honor special occasions.

The SHASTA

Most Shasta villages were along one of the many rivers in northwestern California. Each village had wood-and-dirt houses in which one or more families lived. Big villages had a large house for group meetings and a **sweathouse**. Several villages formed a band led by a headman.

The Shasta held **ceremonies** when boys and girls turned 12. There were more ceremonies for war and hunting parties. Women and men sang and danced, sometimes for several nights!

Shasta village sweathouses were only for men and would have been much like this Hupa sweathouse. Men and boys over about age 12 often slept there until they got married!

TELL ME MORE

The Shasta wore clothing made from deerskin. Bearskins and raccoon skins were also used to make robes and blankets.

The OHLONE

The Ohlone (oh-LOHN-ee) moved according to the season. That way, they were able to hunt, fish, and gather all year long. Every so often, they burned off brush and plants on part of their land. Burning helped the natural grasses grow and made food for the deer and elk.

Respecting each other was an important part of Ohlone life. Everyone shared food and goods, so no one was a lot richer or poorer than anyone else. People took care of each other when they were sick.

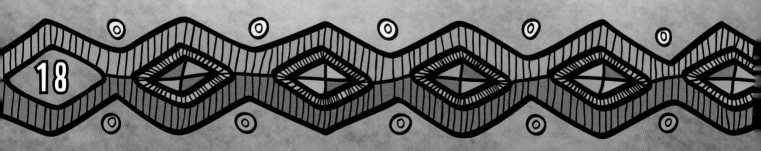

The 50 Ohlone groups lived in homes like this one around the San Francisco Bay area and as far south as Monterey Bay.

TELL ME MORE

The Ohlone ate all the animals in the area, including bugs, lizards, mice, and birds. They also ate roots, seeds, and acorns.

The CHUMASH

The Chumash were talented canoe builders. Their watertight canoes allowed them to paddle from the mainland to the islands off the California coast. They could travel to other Chumash villages on the coast, too. A chief, who could be a man or a woman, headed each village.

The Chumash showed the swordfish special honor. They believed it was the chief of the sea animals. They even performed a Swordfish Dance! The Chumash believed swordfish could make whales swim onto their beach for food.

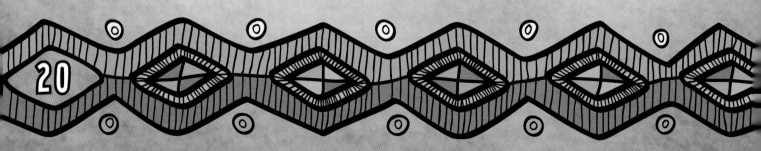

The Chumash made cave paintings of people and animals. Today, the National Park Service takes care of these priceless works of art.

TELL ME MORE

The Swordfish Dancers of the past wore the skull of a real swordfish on their head.

21

New Spanish SETTLEMENTS

In the late 1760s, Spanish soldiers traveled from Mexico to California and built towns. Father Junípero Serra and later Catholic priests built 21 **missions**.

Spanish and Mexican colonists, soldiers, and native peoples lived in the missions. The native peoples weren't treated well. They were forced to give up their **traditional** clothes, language, beliefs, and food. They worked hard and weren't allowed to return to their homelands. They had to **convert** to the Catholic faith. Many died from European illnesses.

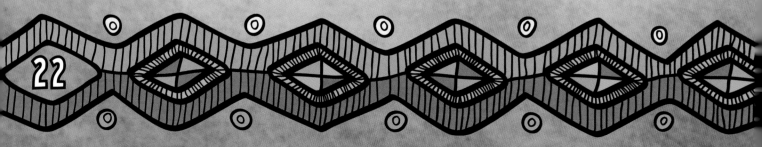

The Spanish thought they were making the lives of Native Americans better by building the missions. The native peoples encountered many hardships, however, including European illnesses their bodies couldn't fight.

TELL ME MORE

The native peoples didn't use the name "California." The Spanish named the land after a make-believe island in a book.

The United States EXPANDS

After a war with Mexico, the Spanish left California. Many native Californians were still forced to work at missions, and the Mexican government gave their homelands to ranchers. Illnesses continued to reduce the native population.

In 1847, the United States took over California. Gold was discovered there soon after. The gold seekers and settlers took even more native land. Native peoples were then moved to special lands set aside for them called reservations. Many didn't want to go.

From November 1969 to June 1971, a group of native Californians started living on Alcatraz Island near San Francisco Bay. They claimed the land based on an agreement native groups had made with the US government in 1868.

UNITED INDIAN PROPERTY
ALCATRAZ ISLAND AREA 12 ACRES
1½ MILES TO TRANSPORT DOCK
ONLY GOVERNMENT BOATS PERMITTED
OTHERS MUST KEEP OFF 200 YARDS
NO LAND ALLOWED ASHORE
WITHOUT A PASS

INDIAN LAND

TELL ME MORE

In the early 1900s, the native groups in California began fighting for their rights. Around this time, their numbers started to rise again, too.

Native Groups of California TODAY

The US government recognizes 109 native groups in California today, and more are waiting to be recognized. Each has its own government. There are almost 100 reservations. Members of a tribe can live there, but they don't have to.

The government allows the reservations to have **casinos**. The money from these casinos helps the reservations improve the way of life for Native Americans. Many are able to have better jobs, food, housing, and health care.

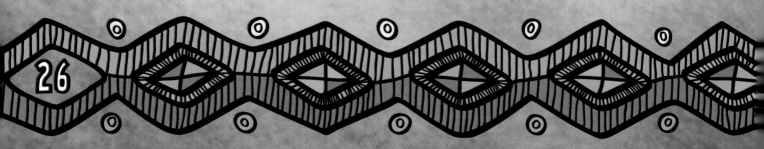

RESERVATIONS OF CALIFORNIA

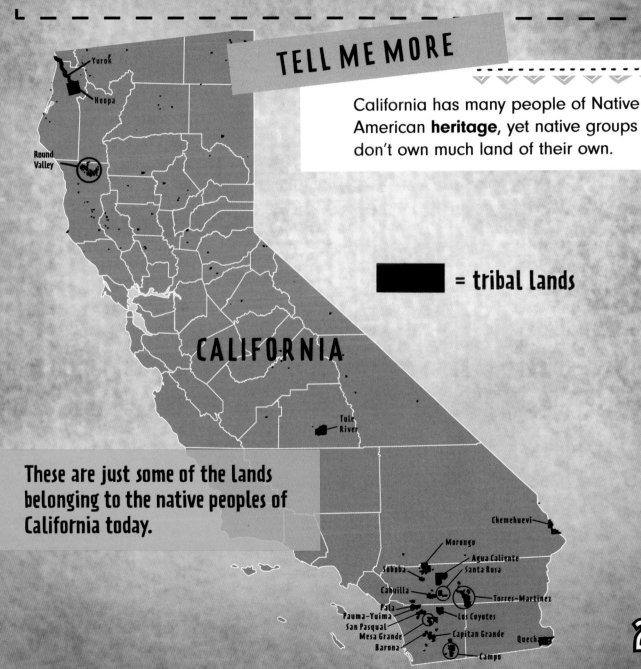

TELL ME MORE

California has many people of Native American **heritage**, yet native groups don't own much land of their own.

= tribal lands

These are just some of the lands belonging to the native peoples of California today.

Yurok

Hoopa

Round Valley

CALIFORNIA

Tule River

Chemehuevi

Morongo

Agua Caliente

Soboba

Santa Rosa

Cahuilla

Torres-Martinez

Pala

Los Coyotes

Pauma-Yuima

San Pasqual

Mesa Grande

Capitan Grande

Barona

Campo

Quechan

Come to a POWWOW!

A powwow is a celebration of Native American heritage and tradition. There are several powwows a year in California. They're usually free and open to the public. Here's what you can see and do:

- watch dances
- listen to drums
- sing songs
- listen to stories

- taste traditional, yummy foods, such as fry bread
- buy beautiful, handmade crafts
- make your own basket, necklace, or other craft

Many native groups have websites. You can check them to find out the dates and locations of powwows and other events!

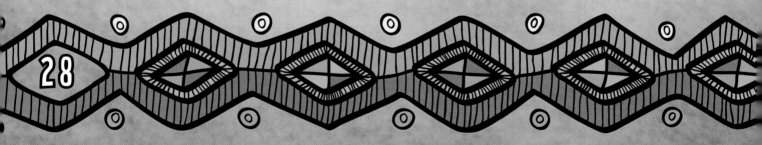

Going to a powwow is a great way to honor the culture of native peoples.

29

GLOSSARY

archaeologist: a person who digs up objects and remains of buildings to learn about life in the past

boundary: something that marks the limit of an area or place

casino: a place where people play games of chance to try to win money

ceremony: an event to honor or celebrate something

convert: to change one's religion to another religion

design: the pattern or shape of something

heritage: something that comes from past members of a family or group

leak: to let water or other liquids out

mainland: a large piece of land that makes up most of a country or other landmass

migrate: to move from one country or area to another

mission: a church started in a foreign country to teach about religion

sweathouse: a hut heated by steam often made by pouring water over hot stones

traditional: having to do with long-practiced ways of life

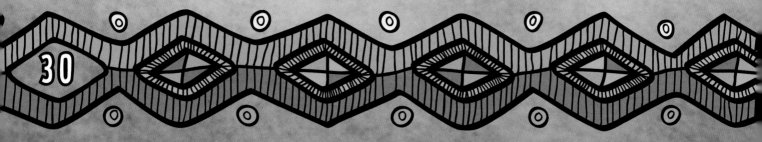

For More INFORMATION

Books

eKids Press. *Meet the Chumash Native American Tribe!* Anaheim, CA: Minute Help Press, 2012.

Gimpel, Diane Marczely. *A Timeline History of Early American Indian Peoples.* Minneapolis, MN: Lerner Publications, 2015.

Sonneborn, Liz. *California Indians.* Chicago, IL: Heinemann Library, 2012.

Websites

California Indians: Making a Difference

californiamuseum.org/california-indians-making-difference

Take a virtual tour of this California Museum exhibit to learn more about California's native peoples.

California Indians in Olden Times: Native Americans for Kids

nativeamericans.mrdonn.org/california.html

What would you like to know about the food, clothing, culture, and crafts of California's native peoples? Check out this website to find your answer.

INDEX